**DO NOT REMOVE
CARDS FROM POCKET**

"All the President's Men and Women"

Al Gore
Vice President of the United States

Bob Italia

Published by Abdo & Daughters, 4940 Viking Dr., Suite 622, Edina, MN 55435.

Library bound edition distributed by Rockbottom Books, Pentagon Tower, P.O. Box 36036, Minneapolis, Minnesota 55435.

Cover Photo by: Wide World Photos, Inc.
Inside Photos by: Black Star (5, 7, 13, 18, 19, 20, 21, 25, 26)
Wide World Photos, Inc. (9, 11)
Bettmann Archive (22)

Edited By Rosemary Wallner

Library of Congress Cataloging–in–Publication Data
Italia, Robert, 1955-
    Al Gore : vice president of the United States / Bob Italia.
        p.   cm — (All the President's men and women)
    Includes bibliographical references and index.
    Summary: Describes the life and career of the politician who has been called the "Environmental Vice–President."
    ISBN 1-56239-253-0 (lib. bdg.)
    1. Gore, Albert, 1946—Juvenile literature. 2. Vice–Presidents—United States—Biography—Juvenile literature.
    [1. Gore, Albert, 1946–. 2. Vice–Presidents.] I. Title. II. Series.
E840.8.G65I84   1993
973.929' 092—dc20   93-26099
    [B]   CIP
                                                               AC

CONTENTS

The Environmental Vice President

At one time, Democratic Senator Al Gore wanted to be President of the United States. He ran for the office in 1988, but people did not think he was warm or friendly. After his defeat in the New York primary, Gore withdrew from the race. He devoted more of his time to family and causes like the environment.

Then in 1992, Bill Clinton chose Al Gore as his running mate. After the election, Gore found himself in the second-highest office in America.

Gore has important plans for the environment. He wants to stop wasteful energy use and exploitation of natural resources. With Bill Clinton's support, Gore should prove to be an influential member of the president's cabinet while establishing policies that help clean up America.

The Senator's Son

Albert Arnold (Al) Gore, Jr., was born on March 31, 1948, in Washington, D.C. His father is former Senator Al Gore, Sr. His mother, Pauline Gore, is a lawyer. His sister, Nancy, was 10 years older than Gore. She often helped Gore's father with his campaigns.

Because Albert, Sr., worked in Washington, D.C., Gore spent half of each year in the Fairfax Hotel on Massachusetts Avenue. The Fairfax was a residential hotel owned by a Gore relative.

*Al Gore delivers a speech at the Democratic
National Convention, July 1992.*

During holidays and for most of the summer, the Gores returned to Tennessee. But his parents spent most of their time making public appearances and speeches to keep in touch with the voters. When he was five years old, Gore was left in the care of Alota and William Thompson. They were tenant farmers who ran the Gores' farm outside Carthage, a small town about 50 miles east of Nashville.

The Thompson home had no indoor plumbing. A single coal-burning fireplace heated the house. Al shared a bed with the Thompsons' only child, Gordon. Alota, a nurse, became a second mother to Gore. "She loved him as much as she did me," Gordon recalled years later. Gore became so attached to the Thompsons, he often demanded to stay with them whenever his parents were not around.

Gore became interested in politics at a young age. He often sat in front of the television to watch the political conventions. "[Gore] was real interested in it," Gordon said. "He knew a lot about politics even when he was small."

Gore attended St. Albans High School in Washington. (St. Albans is one of the nation's most exclusive schools.) In the summer, Gore returned to Carthage to work in the corn fields with friends.

Senator Albert Gore, Sr.

Tipper

At a graduation party, Gore met May Elizabeth Aitcheson. May's nickname was Tipper. Her mother had named her after a character in a nursery rhyme. Tipper was outgoing and warm. She had attended private schools all her life. Her grandfather was a prominent banker.

After a few dates, Gore and Aitcheson began talking about marriage. Al invited Tipper to his parents' farm to meet his family. When she came to breakfast one morning in a dress and make-up instead of casual clothing, she charmed Gore's parents. Because Tipper was so charming, Gore knew then that she was the right woman for him.

In 1966, Gore attended Harvard University in Boston, Massachusetts. He thought he would become a writer or a lawyer-journalist. Gore was interested in making the world a better place to live. He thought that a career in writing or journalism could help him change things for the better. Through his writing, Gore felt he could make people aware of the world's problems.

Gore spent one summer working as an office boy at the *New York Times*. He traveled less and less to Carthage. He and Tipper talked about making movies and living by the sea. She would paint and he would write. But their dreams took a different turn.

*Tipper Gore holds a small child during a dedication
ceremony for New York City's Sojourner Truth House.*

The Vietnam Issue

After he graduated in 1969 with a bachelor's degree in government, Gore joined the Army—even though he opposed the Vietnam War. He feared that avoiding the draft would hurt his father's 1970 re-election chances. But he also wanted to make sure that no boyhood friend of his from Carthage would go to war in his place.

While in the army, Gore campaigned hard for his father. He even posed in his army uniform with his father. But his father did not win re-election to the Senate. Gore was disappointed that his campaigning did not get his father re-elected. It was one of the few times, Pauline Gore recalled, that she had ever seen her son cry.

After the election, Gore married Tipper. Then he was sent to Vietnam. Because of his writing talents, Gore got a job as an army journalist. Throughout his army career, Gore remained opposed to the Vietnam War. But he put in his time. He felt the military was an obligation, even though he thought that America should not be involved in the war. During his time in Vietnam, Gore never saw combat.

When Gore returned from Vietnam, his interest in politics had soured. He and Tipper moved to the country near Carthage to live a simple life. From 1971 to 1972, Gore took graduate courses in religion at Vanderbilt University Divinity School in Tennessee. There, he took time to sort out his feelings about the war. "I think it was a purification," Tipper recalled.

Maya Lin, designer of the Vietnam Veterans Memorial, and Vice President-elect Al Gore participate in Veterans Day ceremonies at the Memorial in Washington, D.C. (November 1992).

Gore decided he no longer had any interest in politics. His parents tried to coax him into attending Democratic Party functions, but he declined. He was perfectly happy raising a family. In 1972, the Gores had their first child, Karenna.

While studying religion, Gore became a reporter at *The Tennessean* in Nashville. In 1974, he entered Vanderbilt Law School. But he continued writing for the newspaper and never earned his law degree.

Running for Congress

Gore was still interested in changing the world for the better. But he gradually began to think that real power would only come by holding political office.

John Seigenthaler was the publisher of *The Tennessean*. He was also a major force in state Democratic politics. In 1976, he called Gore on the telephone and told him that the Carthage Congressional job would be up for election. Gore was interested.

Gore hung up the telephone, turned to Tipper and said, "I think I'm going to run for Congress." He immediately dropped to the floor and began doing push-ups. He wanted to get in shape for the race.

"It just came home to me that if I was ever going to do it," Gore recalled, "now was the time. Not 10 years from now. Now."

Gore asked his father not to get involved in the election. He wanted to earn the job by himself. Once elected, Gore and his family moved to Arlington, Virginia. He bought the house that Tipper had lived in as a girl and settled into his new life as a political figure.

Gore proved to be a hard worker. He had learned a valuable lesson from his father's election defeat: don't lose touch with the people. Gore returned to Tennessee often to hold weekend town meetings. During these meetings, Gore talked to people about the issues that were important to them. "He was a better listener than I ever was," his father said.

In Congress, Gore wanted to attain a position of influence. Soon, he was holding hearing about toxic waste and other environmental issues. As a former reporter, he knew what made a good story. He got more than his share of headlines—and critics.

Al Gore campaigns with his wife, Tipper (July 1992).

Senator Gore

By 1982, Gore had four children; Karenna, Kristen, Sarah, and Albert III. In 1984, he ran for the U.S. Senate and won. But before he found out he had won, his sister, Nancy, died of lung cancer. Nancy had been involved in Gore's four Congressional campaigns and his successful run for Senate. She died without ever knowing he had won.

In 1988, a group of powerful Democratic fund-raisers urged Gore to run for the presidency. Eager for a higher office, Gore agreed. But the press criticized Gore for his unemotional speeches and his tendency to keep his distance from people. When Gore was badly defeated in the New York primary, he withdrew from the race.

Gore was hurt and shocked by the defeat. He had lived a charmed life. He was the son of a famous senator and had a Harvard education. Gore was not used to defeat or rejection.

"I had just lost a presidential election," he said, "having given it everything that I had, and encountered the limits of my capacity to persuade people of policies I felt so deeply needed to be followed."

After the defeat, Gore devoted himself to studying the environment. It was an issue he had become interested in soon after entering the House of Representatives. Soon he resumed his normal hectic pace of meetings, hearings, luncheons—and preparations for another possible run for the presidency.

Tragedy

In 1989, tragedy struck on the opening day of baseball season. Gore took his son, Albert III, to a baseball game at Memorial Stadium in Baltimore, Maryland. Outside the stadium after the game, Albert darted in front of a car. The impact knocked Albert 30 feet into the air, then dragged him across the pavement for 20 more feet. By the time Gore reached his son, Albert was lying in the gutter without pulse or breath. His eyes were open in what Gore later described as "the empty stare of death."

As Gore held his son, he fell into deep despair. After his son was hospitalized at Johns Hopkins Children's Center in Baltimore, Gore canceled all his appointments. He and Tipper spent the next month at Albert's side. After many long and painful months that included surgery, his son recovered.

"All these things that had loomed so large," Gore said, "not only in my daily life, but in my whole set of priorities, all of a sudden didn't amount to a hill of beans."

Surprisingly, Gore found that the accident brought him closer to people. "There was an outpouring of empathy and compassion from people I didn't know," he recalled, "from people I did know but didn't really know—people who ran the elevators at the Capitol and the subway car from the Senate Office Building to the Capitol, police officers, janitors, secretaries, staff in the Senate.

"People who I suddenly came to understand had, in many cases, gone through experiences worse than the one my family had gone through and were carrying these heavy burdens in their hearts, without giving any indication outwardly that I had picked up—partly because I wasn't paying attention."

Earth in the Balance

For someone who had learned to keep his emotions locked up, the public's reaction to his suffering became a release. He let his feelings out, and he reexamined his life. In the months that followed, Gore began work on *Earth in the Balance: Ecology and the Human Spirit*. He wrote the book at night in his parents' Capitol Hill apartment. When it was published in January 1992, the book reached the *New York Times* best-seller list.

In the summer of 1991, Gore announced that he would not enter the race for the presidential nomination. "I would like to be president," he said at the time, "but I am also a father. And I feel deeply about my responsibility to my children."

EARTH
IN THE
BALANCE

ECOLOGY AND
THE HUMAN SPIRIT

PLUME

"A powerful summons for the politics of life and hope."—Bill Moyers

VICE PRESIDENT
AL GORE

WITH A NEW FOREWORD

Al Gore's book, Earth in the Balance, *was a best-seller.*

Running with Bill

In May 1992, Warren Christopher, who headed Bill Clinton's vice-presidential search committee, met with Gore. He asked Gore if he was interested in the position of vice president. "It was a very guarded, reluctant response," Christopher stated. "He said that was something he would have to think about for a long time." But Gore did not rule it out.

Al Gore and Bill Clinton shake hands at the Democratic National Convention, July 16, 1992.

One month later, Christopher called Gore in Rio de Janeiro, Brazil. Gore was attending the Earth Summit to discuss the world's environmental problems with representatives of foreign governments. Christopher wanted to know if Gore would be willing to place his name on a short list for nomination. Gore told him he would let him know the following day. As far as Gore was concerned, his son and entire family had healed much during the year he had spent not running for the presidency.

Al Gore waves to the crowd at the Democratic National Convention in New York City (July 1992).

"I thought about it," Gore said. "And I reframed the question to take the personal ambition part out of it, because I didn't want to do it in that sense. I didn't expect it. I didn't seek it. When I said yes, the question to which I answered yes was, 'Were you willing to give your country a better chance to change?'—not 'Do you want to run for vice president?'"

At the National Democratic Convention in July 1992, Gore stood in front of projected images of his son Albert and described the near-fatal accident. Afterward, some critics said that Gore was using his

The Gores and the Clintons celebrate on the final day of the Democratic National Convention.

son's pain and private family issue to further his political career. But the Gores defended the speech.

"That happened to us, in public, and we dealt with it in public," Tipper said. "We kept as much private as we could. But it's become a part of our lives, and it's part of who we are and very much a part of who Al is. I think that it was courageous of him to reveal that. He's a different person in many ways because of that trauma. If you want to know him, you have to know what happened."

Al Gore was enthusiastic about the Democratic Party's chances on Election Day.

Bill Clinton and Al Gore go for an early morning jog in Little Rock (July 10, 1993).

The convention gave Bill Clinton and Al Gore a big boost. A few days later, when polls were taken, the Clinton/Gore ticket soared well past their opponent, President George Bush. Clinton and Gore moved quickly to seize control of the presidential race. Tipper and Al joined Bill and Hillary Clinton on an exhaustive campaign trip across America. The couples rode in buses and stopped in cities and towns, meeting with people. They told everyone of their plans to make America better. During this time, the Gores and the Clintons became close friends.

On November 3, 1993, the Clinton/Gore ticket won the presidential race in a landslide. Al Gore was jubilant, but he knew there were tough days ahead. The nation's economy was sluggish, the national debt was soaring, and there were many people looking for jobs. It would take a lot of hard work to make things better. In January 1993, Al Gore stood on the steps of the nation's Capitol Building. There he took the oath of office.

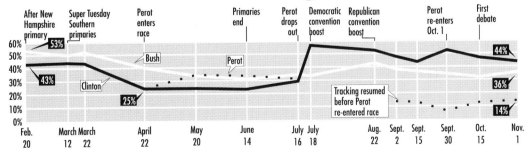

Election 1992: Tracking the Candidates

After the inauguration, the Gores moved into the vice presidential house in Washington, D.C. The 12-acre estate is on the grounds of the Naval Observatory. Though not as fancy as the White House on 1600 Pennsylvania Avenue, it is big enough to raise a family. It also places Gore only a short hop from the White House.

Election '92: How the States Voted

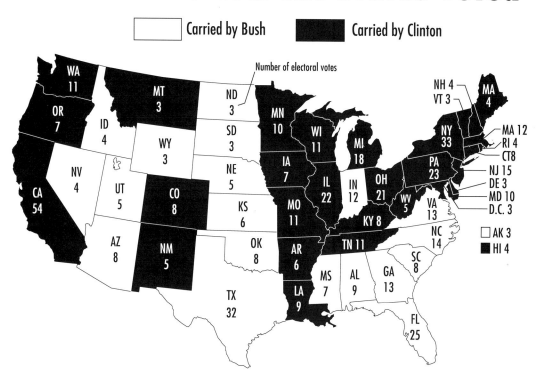

Carried by Bush   Carried by Clinton

Al Gore and Bill Clinton during their bus tour campaign (July 1992).

Keeping Promises

Gore has promised to work hard on behalf of the environment. He will try to steer U.S. government policies away from wasteful energy consumption and exploitation of natural resources. But since Clinton will be under pressure to create new jobs, environmental issues may have to be put on hold. Let's hope that this new generation of political leaders with fresh ideas can help the economy grow without sacrificing the environment.

Al and Tipper Gore are hopeful for the future.

The Office of the Vice President

On September 4, 1787, a committee at the Constitutional Convention recommended that there be an office of vice president. The vice president would be elected in the same manner as the president. He or she would also be the immediate successor to the president in case of death, resignation, removal, or inability of the president to perform his or her duties.

Al Gore is sworn in at the inauguration ceremonies in Washington, D.C. (January 20, 1993).

The U.S. Constitution finally established a four-year term for the vice president. It gave the vice president the duty of overseeing the Senate. It also gave the vice president the power to cast tie-breaking votes. Long ago, the vice president had much influence over the Senate. But these days, the vice president rarely presides over the Senate.

Besides being the immediate successor to the president, today's vice presidents have become an important part of the president's cabinet. A vice president will lend his or her advice, and will preside over the Cabinet if the president is absent.

The vice president is also a member of the National Security Council. The vice president attends meetings between the president and the leaders of Congress. And the vice president represents the president at home and abroad.

Even more, the vice president is the chairperson of the National Aeronautics Space Council and of the Advisory Council of the Peace Corps. Because of the vice president's Constitutional power over the Senate, he or she can help get the president's plans and programs through Congress. Today's vice presidents have truly become an important part of the government.

Glossary

Campaign
A series of actions a person undertakes to attain a political goal.

Debate
A formal discussion or argument.

Deficit
The amount by which a sum of money falls short of the required amount.

Democrat
A member of the Democratic Party.

Economy
The management of a country's resources.

Independent
A person not associated with any established political party.

Media
The means of mass communication, such as newspapers, magazines, radio, and television.

National Debt

The total financial obligations of a national government.

Political Parties

Political organizations, such as the Democratic and Republican parties.

Primary

A meeting of registered voters of a political party for the purpose of nominating candidates.

Republican

A member of the Republican Party.

Connect With Books

Almanac of American Presidents: From 1789 to the Present. Facts on File, 1991.

Alotta, Robert. *A Look at the Vice Presidency.* Julian Messner, 1981.

Beard, Charles Austin. *The Presidents in American History: George Washington to George Bush.* Julian Messner, 1989.

Blassingame, Wyatt. *The Look-It-Up Book of Presidents.* Random House, 1990.

Degregorio, William A. *The Complete Book of U.S. Presidents: From George Washington to George Bush.* Barricade Books (New York), 1991.

Feerick, John D. *The First Book of Vice Presidents.* Franklin Watts, 1977.
The Vice Presidents of the United States. Franklin Watts, 1973.

Freidel, Frank. *The Presidents of the United States of America.* White House Historical Association, 1989.

Lengyel, Cornel Adam. *Presidents of the United States.* Golden Press, 1977.

Parker, Nancy Winslow. *The President's Cabinet and How It Grew.* Harper Collins, 1991.

Powers of the Presidency. *Congressional Quarterly,* 1989.

Index